Arabian Horses

CASKEY

To stay updated on new works,
coloring books and images
Visit
Caskeyart.com

Bethany A. Caskey

ISBN: 9781796981605

I sincerely hope you enjoy this
Arabian Horse Coloring Book.
I have tried to include several levels of
difficulty and a variety of scenes.
Some of the images employ the use of
grayscale, a technique of underpainting used
by the master painters of old to indicate
form and shadows. You will have a chance
to experiment with this coloring technique if
you haven't already as well as many
traditional line drawings.

Suggestions are always welcome.

Happy coloring!!
Bethany Caskey

This Arabian Horse
was colored by:

_____

Date:_____

This Arabian Horse
was colored by:

_____

Date: _____

This Arabian Horse
was colored by:

_____

Date:_____

V.V.V.

CASKEY

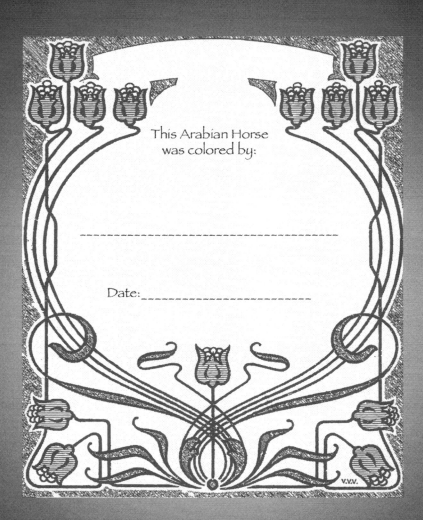

This Arabian Horse
was colored by:

_____

Date: _____

V.V.V.

This Arabian Horse
was colored by:

_____

Date: _____

This Arabian Horse
was colored by:

_____

Date:_____

This Arabian Horse
was colored by:

_____

Date:_____

V.V.

This Arabian Horse
was colored by:

_____

Date:_____

CASKEY

This Arabian Horse
was colored by:

_____

Date:_____

V.V.V.

CASKEY

This Arabian Horse
was colored by:

_____

Date:_____

This Arabian Horse
was colored by:

Date:_____

This Arabian Horse
was colored by:

_____

Date:_____

V.V.

This Arabian Horse
was colored by:

_____

Date: _____

This Arabian Horse
was colored by:

_____

Date:_____

V.V.V.

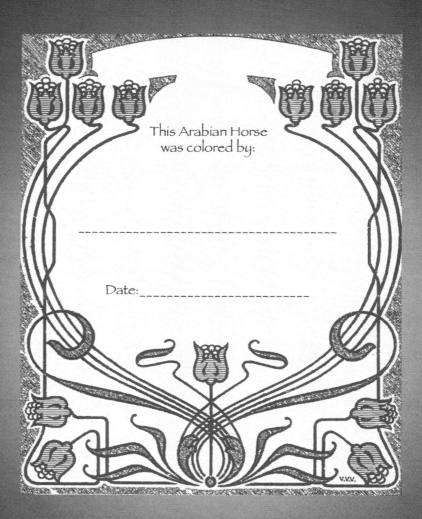

This Arabian Horse
was colored by:

_____

Date:_____

V.V.V.

This Arabian Horse
was colored by:

Date:_____

CASKEY

This Arabian Horse
was colored by:

_____

Date:_____

V.V.

CASKEY

This Arabian Horse
was colored by:

_____

Date:_____

This Arabian Horse
was colored by:

_____

Date:_____

CASKEY

This Arabian Horse
was colored by:

_____

Date:_____

V.V.V.

CASKEY

This Arabian Horse
was colored by:

_____

Date: _____

v.v.v.

This Arabian Horse
was colored by:

_____

Date:_____

This Arabian Horse
was colored by:

_____

Date:_____

V.V.

CASKEY

This Arabian Horse
was colored by:

_____

Date:_____

V.V.V.

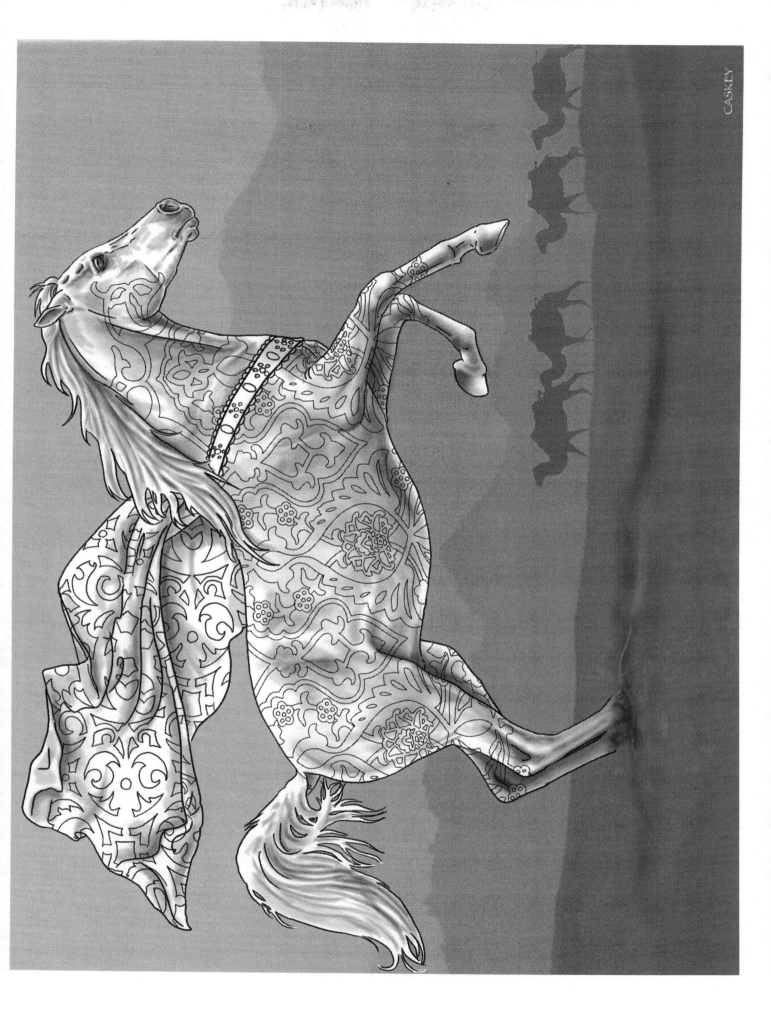

This Arabian Horse
was colored by:

_____

Date:_____

CASKEY

This Arabian Horse
was colored by:

_____

Date:_____

V.V.

This Arabian Horse
was colored by:

_____

Date:_____

This Arabian Horse
was colored by:

_____

Date:_____

CASKEY

This Arabian Horse
was colored by:

Date:_____

CASKEY

This Arabian Horse
was colored by:

_____

Date:_____

This Arabian Horse
was colored by:

_____

Date:_____

V.V.V.

CASKEY

This Arabian Horse
was colored by:

_____

Date: _____

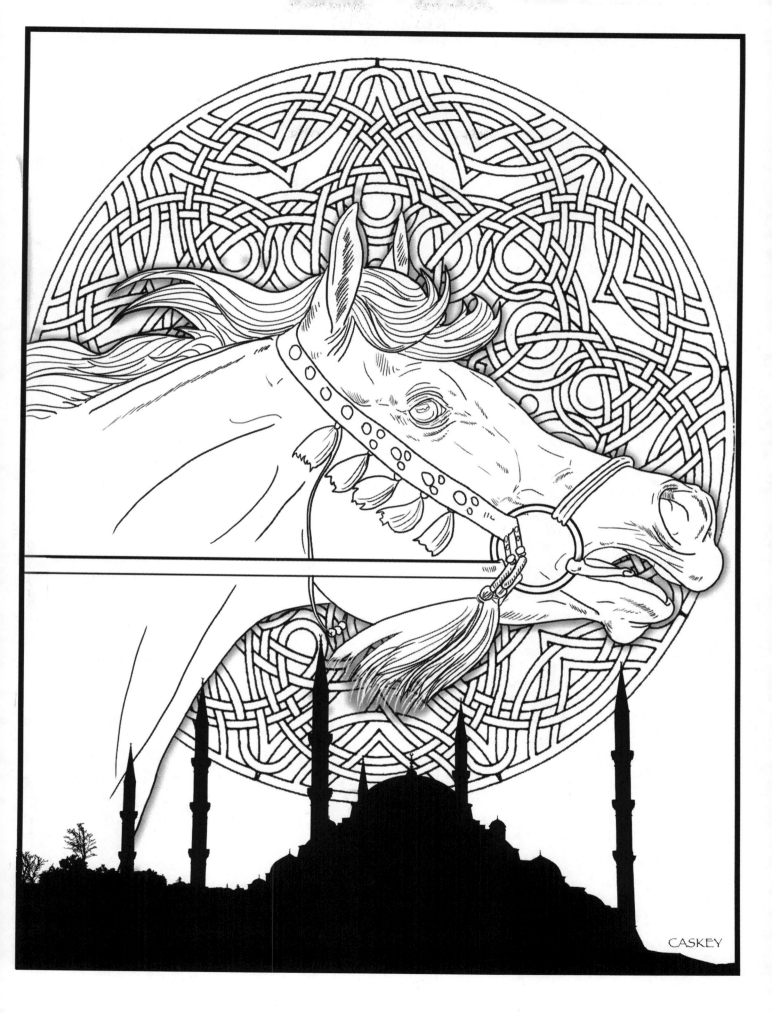

This Arabian Horse
was colored by:

_____

Date:_____

This Arabian Horse
was colored by:

_____

Date:_____

This Arabian Horse
was colored by:

Date:_____

This Arabian Horse
was colored by:

_____

Date:_____

CASKEY

This Arabian Horse
was colored by:

_____

Date:_____

This Arabian Horse
was colored by:

_____

Date:_____

CASKEY

This Arabian Horse
was colored by:

_____

Date:_____

V.V.

"The wind of
Heaven is that which
blows between a
horse's ears."

~Arabian Proverb~

Made in the USA
Las Vegas, NV
14 March 2025

19561545R00050